DOC

# LUBBOCK
## City of Land and Sky

TOWERY PUBLISHING, INC.

▲ Ashton Thornhill

# LUBBOCK
## City of Land and Sky

By Freda McVay & Ashton Thornhill

Corporate profiles by Richard & Penny Mason

Art Direction by Anne Castrodale

◀ Jon O Thompson / JOT Visual Productions

Produced in cooperation with the Lubbock Chamber of Commerce

▲ Jon Q. Thompson / JQT Visual Productions

THE IMPACT OF AGRICULTURE ON THIS GROWING CITY OF 190,000-PLUS CAN BE FOUND IN EVERY DIRECTION, FROM THE RANCHING HERITAGE CENTER ON THE CAMPUS OF TEXAS TECH UNIVERSITY TO A LONE TRACTOR PLOWING A NEARBY FIELD BENEATH LUBBOCK'S PROUD SKYLINE.

**LIBRARY OF CONGRESS CATALOGING-IN-PUBLICATION DATA**

McVay, Freda.
    Lubbock  :  city of land and sky / by Freda McVay ; corporate profiles by Richard and Penny Mason ;  art direction by Anne Castrodale.
      p.    cm. — (Urban tapestry series)
  "Produced in cooperation with the Lubbock Chamber of Commerce."
Includes index.
  ISBN 1-881096-09-2
    1. Lubbock (Tex.)—Pictorial works.  2. Lubbock (Tex.)—Description and travel.  I. Lubbock Chamber of Commerce and Board of City Development.  II. Title.  III. Series.
  F394.L9M38  1994
  976.4'847—dc20                    94-21463
                                     CIP

TOWERY Publishing, Inc.
1835 Union Avenue
Memphis, Tennessee 38104

Publisher: J. Robert Towery
Executive Editor: David Dawson
Senior Editors: Michael C. James, Ken Woodmansee
Articles Editor: Stinson Liles
Profile Art Director: Terri Jones
Technical Director: William H. Towery
Copy Editor: Carlisle Hacker

**ACKNOWLEDGEMENTS**

The author gratefully acknowledges the encouragement and suggestions of friends and family who have shared the growing-up-in-Lubbock experience with me. Special thanks to my brother, Bob Brown, for his suggestions; to my friend, Carol Bogle, who helped in typing the manuscript and captions; and to Dr. Roger Saathoff, director of the School of Mass Communications at Texas Tech University, for his friendship and support.

Most important of all, to my grandchildren, Derek and Sarah, I am dedicating this book, in order to help them understand their Texas roots.

# CONTENTS

"THOSE OF US WHO HAVE LIVED HERE FOR A LIFETIME HAVE COME TO EXPECT LUBBOCK'S OPTIMISTIC SPIRIT. AND WITH EACH PASSING YEAR, IT'S OUR HOPE THAT OUR CHILDREN'S CHILDREN WILL UNDERSTAND THEY HAVE INHERITED A LEGACY FROM MEN AND WOMEN WHO MADE A FETISH OUT OF DETERMINATION AND FIERCE INDEPENDENCE. THE SEEMINGLY ENDLESS SKY AND LAND ARE STILL OUT THERE—WITH NEW CHALLENGES WAITING FOR THE NEXT GENERATION."

A LOOK AT THE CORPORATIONS, BUSINESSES, PROFESSIONAL GROUPS, AND COMMUNITY SERVICE ORGANIZATIONS THAT HAVE MADE THIS BOOK POSSIBLE.

BY FREDA McVAY

THE TIME IT TOOK TO WALK FROM TENTH STREET TO THE OLD WEST TEXAS MUSEUM SEEMED LIKE AN ETERNITY FOR A 10-YEAR-OLD LIVING IN LUBBOCK IN THE 1940S, BUT THE TRIP WAS ALWAYS WORTH IT. Situated on the northeast segment of Memorial Circle on the Texas Tech campus, the museum held forth the promise of great adventure—the chance to travel back in time to the exciting days of cowboys and Indians and pioneers and covered wagons. In the middle of the 20th century, in a town less than 50 years old, most of us actually knew kids whose grandparents had lived in half-dugouts, just like the one reconstructed down in the museum basement.

Later, the best part of the adventure was to stand in the middle of the museum's rotunda, absorbing the "ancient history" of Lubbock as depicted in the Peter Hurd mural on the walls. It wasn't really ancient history, but for a youngster, the visions of men in funny clothes squatting around a campfire, sitting smartly on horseback, or posing in front of wooden frame buildings certainly seemed ancient.

It would be years later before we learned that those early settlers of the Llano Estacado area that would contain Lubbock weren't even the first to settle on the South Plains. Indeed, they were 12,000 years too late to qualify as the original inhabitants. But that was before anyone had heard of the Lubbock Lake Landmark State Historical Park, much less knew the significance of this magnificent archaeological find, which, as it turned out, provided well-preserved evidence of the area's earliest residents. For that matter, we didn't know we were standing on the largest non-mountainous geological formation in North America.

ARTIST PETER HURD'S PAINTINGS OF LUBBOCK'S EARLY-DAY EMPIRE BUILDERS (ABOVE) IMMORTALIZED THE PIONEERS WHO FIRST ENVISIONED A THRIVING COMMUNITY ON THE SOUTH PLAINS OF THE TEXAS PANHANDLE.

PAGES 8 & 9:
LUBBOCK'S DEPENDENCE ON BOTH THE LAND AND SKY IS EVER PRESENT, AS ANXIOUS FARMERS KEEP ONE EYE ON THE SOIL AND ONE ON THE HORIZON, LOOKING FOR SIGNS OF THUNDERHEADS THAT CAN BRING A MUCH-NEEDED RAIN.
PHOTOS BY AL HENDERSON (P.8) AND HARVEY MADISON/MADISON PHOTOGRAPHY (P.9)

In fact, most of us growing up in Lubbock back then didn't even really know who Peter Hurd was, except that he was the artist who painted the circular mural of those men in funny clothes. Years later, Hurd would paint the controversial "official portrait" of President Lyndon B. Johnson, which Johnson promptly described as "the ugliest thing I ever saw." Obviously, the 36th president didn't appreciate the talents of the artist who immortalized the most important men of early-day Lubbock.

And what a diverse group they were, those men in the mural: banker C. E. Maedgen, freighter Walter S. Posey, circuit rider Robert F. Dunn, lawyer William H. Bledsoe, merchant Crone W. Furr, civic leader and future Texas Tech president Clifford B. Jones, oilman Sid Richardson, stock farmer Daniel R. Couch, teacher Marcy M. Dupre, cattleman William E. Halsell, cowboy Sam S. Arnett, town builder Marion V. Brownfield, journalist James L. Dow, and chroniclers J. Evetts Haley, Tom Lea, W. Curry Holder, John A. Lomax, and Peter Hurd himself.

These were the men who had the vision of what it would take to transform one of the last settled regions in the United

HURD'S ROTUNDA MURAL WAS THE FOCAL POINT OF THE OLD WEST TEXAS MUSEUM. NOW KNOWN AS THE MUSEUM OF TEXAS TECH, THE ORIGINAL MUSEUM BUILDING HAS BEEN EXPANDED AND RENAMED HOLDEN HALL.

watchful eye—and sometimes heavy hand—was on the pulse of the city.

He and the other Empire Builders—Sam Arnett, Roy Furr, S. E. Cone, A. B. Davis, W. A. Posey, and Parker Prouty, to name but a few—also selected candidates for city and county offices, a practice that fell into disfavor as the city grew. Eventually, handpicked candidates became as obsolete as handpicked cotton; nonetheless, many of the pet projects that began as dreams of the Empire Builders became realities over the next 70 years.

 TANDING BEFORE THE PETER HURD MURAL IN THE OLD MUSEUM, IT WOULD seem that Lubbock was a town consisting entirely of Anglo-Americans. And growing up between Fourth and Nineteenth streets, Avenue Q, and College Avenue, that was the only Lubbock we knew.

But as we got older we discovered that there were several other communities within the city limits, each making its own contribution to the diversity of culture and heritage that is Lubbock today.

The black community was led by dedicated pioneer teachers like E. C. Struggs and Miss Mae Simmons, a grand lady who came to command the respect of all who knew her on both sides of town. The medical needs of that community were met by the late Dr. Joe Chatman, who founded the first hospital/clinic to serve the needs of the city's black residents. A legend in his own time, Dr. Chatman also earned the respect of all Lubbockites with his wry sense of humor and strong sense of decency. He loved to talk about the Depression days, describing a time when his fees might be paid with "a sack of oats or a couple of chickens."

IN SPITE OF THE AREA'S NATURAL EMPHASIS ON CASH CROPS, MANY OF THE PLANTS THAT GROW ON THE PLAINS ARE APPRECIATED AS MUCH FOR THEIR AESTHETICS AS FOR THEIR USEFULNESS.

Years later, old Joe Chatman must have smiled down from whatever lofty perch he had earned up above when the avenue called "Quirt" was officially renamed Martin Luther King Jr. Boulevard. Arm in arm, an entourage of blacks, browns, and whites from all walks of life marched triumphantly down the boulevard, helping to erase any vestige of animosity between the races.

Another community-within-a-community had a parallel history in Lubbock. The town's Hispanic population grew rapidly in response to the increasing demand for migrant

workers to cultivate and harvest the only true "royalty" of the South Plains— "King Cotton." It was these Mexican nationals who were most responsible for getting the raw cotton to the gins for processing.

Over the years, descendants of these early immigrants became leaders in Lubbock, the state of Texas, and throughout the nation. Jose Ramirez became the first Mexican-American elected to the Lubbock School Board; Froy Salinas was the first Mexican-American ever sent by Lubbock to the Texas Legislature; and Lauro Cavazos, the first Hispanic to become president of Texas Tech University, later was tapped as Secretary of Education during the Reagan administration.

ROWING UP, MOST OF US HAD THE DISTINCT IMPRESSION THAT THERE WAS NO OTHER MUSIC IN THE WORLD BUT COUNTRY-AND-WESTERN — AN IMPRESSION FUELED OVER THE DECADES BY THE successes of area musicians such as Bob Wills, Roy Orbison, Jimmy Dean, and, later, Waylon Jennings. But in the 1950s along came Buddy Holly, who took his country music roots and

cultivated a new sound—a sound that made him a rock-and-roll legend.

Since then, Lubbock has become home to a variety of musical styles. The Lubbock Symphony Orchestra, founded by Bill Harrod, has delighted Lubbockites for decades. Texas Tech's "Goin' Band from Raiderland" marches smartly in local parades and often steals the show at Tech football games. The wonderful variety of music options brought to town by the old Lubbock Music Club—and, more recently, the Tech Artist Series—has introduced the town to the sounds of classical masters. And several lively nightspots feature some of the best country-and-western acts in the world, as well as rock-and-roll and rhythm-and-blues.

Indeed, for those of us who remember sneaking liquor in brown paper bags into the old Cotton Club, listening to Tommy Hancock and the Roadside Playboys, Lubbock's nightlife today seems like New York City.

NOTED COLUMNIST MOLLY IVINS ONCE SAID THAT LUBBOCK IS 88.3 PERCENT SKY. FEW WHO HAVE EXPERIENCED THE WIDE-OPEN FEEL OF THE CITY WOULD ARGUE WITH HER CLAIM.

Which brings us to one of the great ironies of modern-day Lubbock—the success of the fledgling but burgeoning wine industry. Most of us remember when hometowners bragged that Lubbock was the largest city in the United States to be completely "dry"—and they weren't talking about the weather. When an occasional liquor election was held, the "wets" and "drys" fought tooth and nail in the pages of the newspaper, from the pulpits of the town's numerous churches, and on the streets with pamphlets and, sometimes, fists.

As both Texas Tech and Reese Air Force Base grew, bringing more and more newcomers to the area, community attitudes slowly changed. The progression went from the old brown-bag days to "private clubs" (you paid a dollar at the

THE SIGHT OF JUICY RED TOMATOES *at the local farmers markets is a sure sign that summer has arrived.*

*LUBBOCK IS DEDICATED TO PRE-serving the past in order to secure a bright future. A perfect example is the Depot District. Beginning with the conversion of the old railroad depot into a fashionable restaurant, renovations continue in one of the oldest sections in town.*

AFTER ESTABLISHING THE DEPOT *Restaurant and Depot Beer Garden, promoters opened the 19th Street Warehouse, which features live music from both local and touring bands.*

IN A STATE THAT'S RENOWNED FOR *its barbecue, no place enjoys a finer reputation than the legendary Stubb's restaurant, which was moved from its original site on East Broadway to the Depot District, near downtown. Depot District "works in progress" include more new restaurants, live music venues, a micro-brewery, and a performance theater.*

MUSIC REMAINS AN INTEGRAL PART *of life in Lubbock, and everything from country and blues to rock and jazz can be heard in local clubs and concert halls.*

NESTLED AMONG NEWER BUILDINGS, *the historic Pioneer Hotel has also served as a high-rise retirement center, one of the numerous senior citizen facilities scattered throughout the city.*

ANOTHER DOWNTOWN LUBBOCK *landmark is the old Lindsey Theater, once the most popular theater in West Texas. While other movie houses could charge only 35 cents a ticket, the majestic Lindsey, with its plush red carpet and classic staircase, could command 50 cents— and sometimes 75 cents—for admission to a first-run feature.*

A UNIQUE FEATURE OF THE CITY *streets between downtown and the Texas Tech campus is the red-brick roads built during the Depression, when manpower was cheap and materials were readily available.*

OF ALL THE BUILDINGS THAT *instill pride for longtime Lubbock-ites, none tugs at the heartstrings more than Lubbock High School. With its Spanish architecture and halls full of memories, the school is now a Texas historic landmark. At one time, LHS boasted the longest hall of any public high school in the state.*

EVEN LUBBOCK'S NEWER BUILD-ings, *such as NationsBank at the 19th Street corner of the Texas Tech campus, reflect the ranching and farming heritage of the city and surrounding area.*

EXTRACTING OIL—THE OTHER *"cash crop"* of Texas—out of the ground and transporting it to refineries has developed into a sophisticated, highly technical process.

▲ MARK C. MAMAWAL

**PAGES 48 & 49:**
**THANKS TO THE WEALTH OF COTTON**
*gins and other related businesses*
*in Lubbock, the region's $1 billion*
*cotton crop has an economic impact*
*of $3 billion on the city's economy.*
**PHOTO BY ASHTON THORNHILL**

WHEN IT COMES TO LUBBOCK-AREA *agribusiness, cotton is king. Twenty-five percent of the cotton produced in the United States is grown on the High Plains of Texas.*

ALMOST HALF OF THE GRAPES grown in Texas are produced in the rich soil around Lubbock, where grape growing and wine production have become big business.

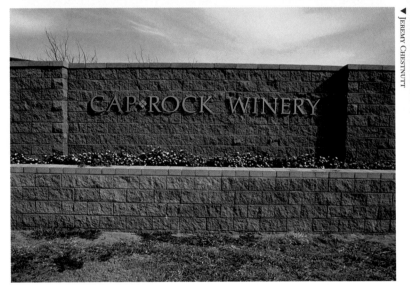

**LUBBOCK'S THREE MAJOR WINERIES** *have been recognized both nationally and internationally for their outstanding products. Pheasant Ridge Winery, named for the abundance of pheasants in the area, modeled itself after a European-style vineyard. Cap✦Rock Winery, which took its name from the geological formations beneath the city, uses the most advanced equipment available in its wine-making process. Llano Estacado Winery has won more awards than any other winery in Texas.*

WITH FIVE MAJOR AIR CARRIERS, *Lubbock International Airport sees more than 40 flights arrive and depart daily, connecting the city to the rest of the world (top, left and right). Sitting on 3,000 acres, the airport is an official U.S. Customs Port of Entry and serves more than a half-million boardings annually.*

ALSO DOTTING THE SKIES ARE *training planes from Reese Air Force Base, one of the top 10 employers in Lubbock (bottom, left and right). Established in World War II as Lubbock Army Air Field, Reese enjoys one of the best Air Force/ community relationships in the nation.*

LUBBOCK'S WEALTH OF PUBLIC *services are available from sunrise to sunset and beyond. In addition to top-rated fire and police protection, transportation services include the Citibus mass transit system and the T.N.M.& O. bus line, both of which connect Lubbock to the rest of the region.*

"WALK OF FAME"

LUBBOCK AND THE WEST TEXAS AREA ARE RICH IN HERITAGE AND CONTRIBUTIONS FROM MANY GIFTED PEOPLE IN THE FIELD OF MUSIC AND ENTERTAINMENT. TO PRESERVE AND SHARE THIS RICH HERITAGE, THE LUBBOCK "WALK OF FAME" WAS DEDICATED SEPTEMBER 6, 1980.

CIVIC LUBBOCK, INC.
1983

IN LOVING MEMORY OF OUR OWN
BUDDY HOLLEY
SEPTEMBER 7, 1936
FEBRUARY 3, 1959

LEGENDARY LUBBOCK MUSICIAN *Buddy Holly is memorialized not only in bronze, but also in the living memory of those who knew him, like Jake Goss, Holly's onetime barber (opposite).*

BUDDY HOLLY EXPLODED ONTO *the national music scene to become a major influence on rock and roll. The Holly Recreation Area in Lubbock and the accompanying Walk of Fame (left) pay homage to Holly's artistic contributions as well as those of other Lubbock-area musicians.*

*Commemorating the tragic day in 1959 when Buddy Holly met his untimely death in a plane crash, fans from throughout the world visit his grave each year (bottom left).*

SINCE THE FIRST "SIGHTING" IN 1988, *thousands of faithful Catholics have gathered each year to view what they believe to be the miracu-* *lous apparition of the Virgin Mary in the sky above St. John Neumann Catholic Church in west Lubbock.*

AMONG THE MOST MAGNIFICENT *of the local Methodist churches is historic First United Methodist in downtown Lubbock. The spectacular stained glass windows are admired by worshipers throughout the South Plains.*

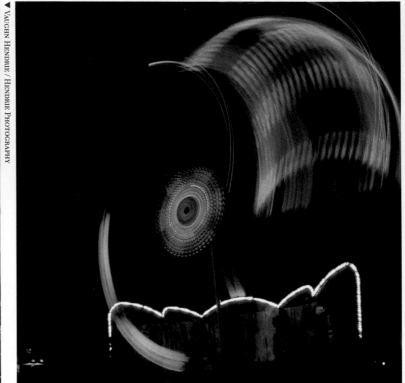

ONE OF THE OLDEST OF LUBBOCK'S
*annual events is the Panhandle
South Plains Fair. In addition to
the colorful midway rides, the fair's
food, livestock, music, and exhibits
light up the atmosphere each fall.*

THE OFFICIAL SEAL OF TEXAS TECH University (opposite), at the Broadway entrance to the campus, is the most popular site for "photo ops" of graduates and their parents.

The largest state-supported university in the United States in terms of acreage, Texas Tech can best be viewed in its entirety from the air.

FROM AN ORIGINAL STUDENT BODY
*of less than 1,000, Texas Tech has
become a multipurpose university
serving more than 24,000 students
and a faculty and staff of more
than 6,500.*

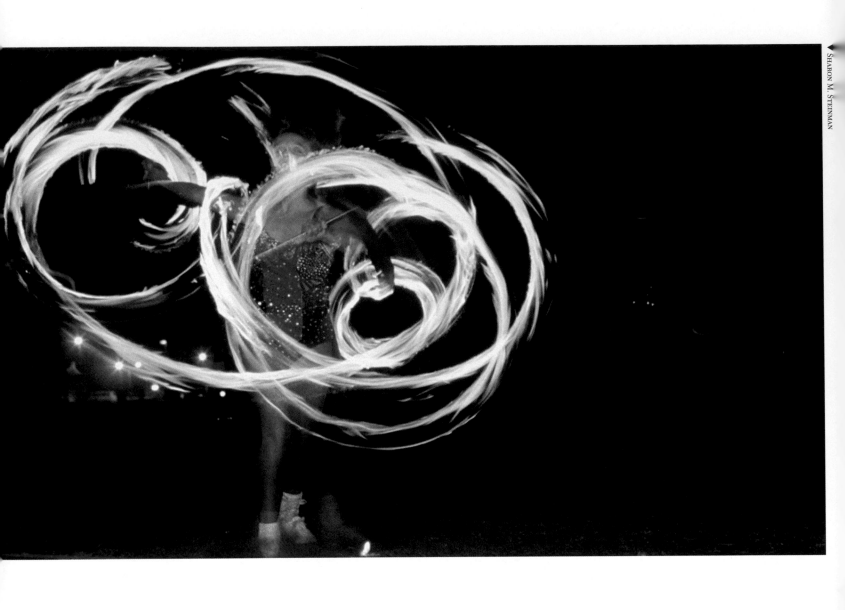

82

SCHOOL SPIRIT ABOUNDS AT TEXAS
*Tech and frequently contributes*
*spectacular sights and sounds. In*
*addition to the traditional bonfire,*
*the ringing of the Victory Bell—in*
*the tower of the original administra-*
*tion building—signals every football*
*triumph.*

CONSIDERED AN ARCHITECTURAL
*showpiece in the Southwest, the
Texas Tech campus follows a
traditional Spanish architectural
theme, including adobe-colored
bricks and red-tile roofs.*

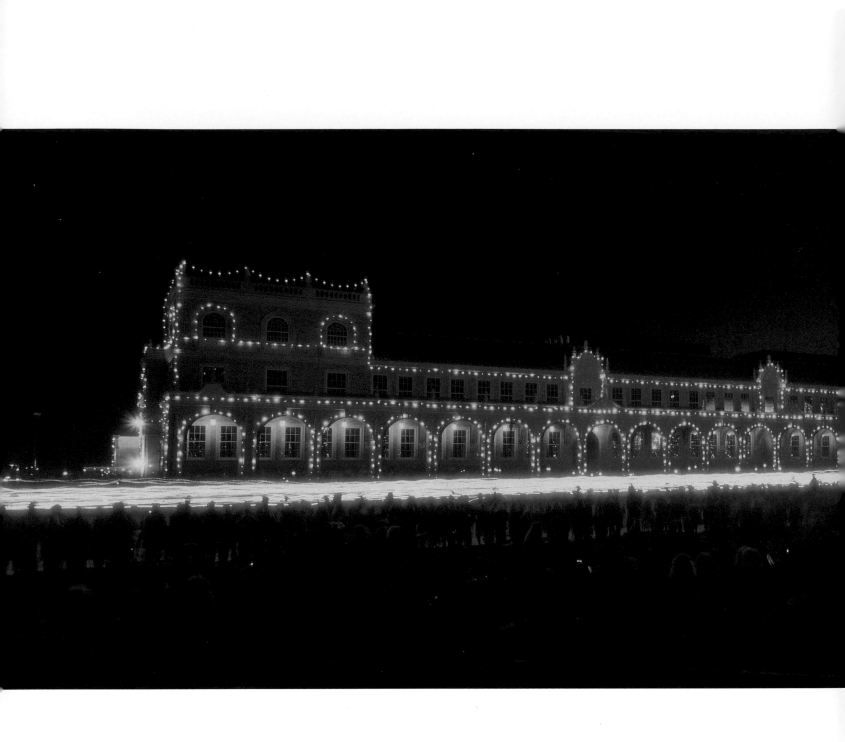

FEW TRADITIONS AT TEXAS TECH *are more sacred than the annual Carol of Lights festival, which kicks off the Christmas season and sets the tone for both the campus and the community as a whole. Workers spend weeks in the fall outlining* *all of the buildings on Memorial Circle in preparation for the annual event. The nightly display illuminates the Christmas season from early December through the first week in January.*

PHOTO BY ARTIE LIMMER

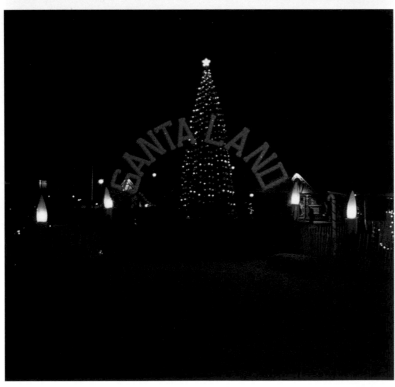

**HOMEOWNERS THROUGHOUT**
*Lubbock go all out during the*
*Christmas season, and many homes*
*are featured in annual tours. In*
*addition, local yule festivals include*
*Santaland near downtown, and the*
*community Christmas party at the*
*Lubbock Memorial Civic Center*
*(above), highlighted by visits from*
*Santa Claus and Pancho Claus.*

▲ SHARON M. STEINMAN

DIE-HARD SUBJECTS OF KING FOOT-
*ball found themselves welcoming a
new member to the court when
Queen Basketball suddenly took
over the limelight in the early 1990s.
Coach Marsha Sharp became the
focus of the city's attention when
her Lady Raiders won the national
championship, led by national
player of the year Sheryl Swoops.*

   *Coach Sharp brought more than
the national championship trophy
back to Texas Tech; she also brought
a new respectability to all of the
school's women's athletic programs.*

TEXAS TECH STUDENTS ARE NEVER *too busy to make a few signs to flash during a big game. Even Governor Ann Richards, a longtime supporter of women's athletics, gets a personal reminder of the Lady Red Raider's victory over UT Austin during Tech's march to the national championship in 1993.*

ANOTHER TEXAS TECH SPORT
*growing in popularity is women's
volleyball, which is led by former
Southwest Conference Coach of
the Year Mike Jones. Successful
women's golf and tennis teams will
be enhanced with the addition of
women's soccer, started in 1994.*

TEXAS TECH BASEBALL HAS COME *into its own in the last few seasons under coach Larry Hays. Consistent winning seasons have attracted a growing number of spectators to Dan Law Field.*

THE TEXAS TECH AQUATIC
*Center features a removable top
that keeps swimmers protected in
the winter and warm beneath the
West Texas sun in the summer.*

*Stacy Balen of the Lubbock High
swimming team practices for an
upcoming meet (bottom).*

ALTHOUGH WEST TEXAS AND *water sports may not seem compatible, the area's larger playa lakes are dotted with wind-surfers throughout the summer—and there's plenty of West Texas wind to keep them going.*

THERE ARE A LOT OF WAYS TO *get where you're going in West Texas, and Lubbockites enjoy cycling, waterskiing, riding go-carts, horseback riding, and countless other outdoor activities.*

A HOSPITABLE CLIMATE IS ONE OF
the many reasons for the popularity
of golf on the South Plains. In
addition to the five public courses
and three country clubs in Lubbock,
dozens of courses are available
within an hour's drive in any
direction.

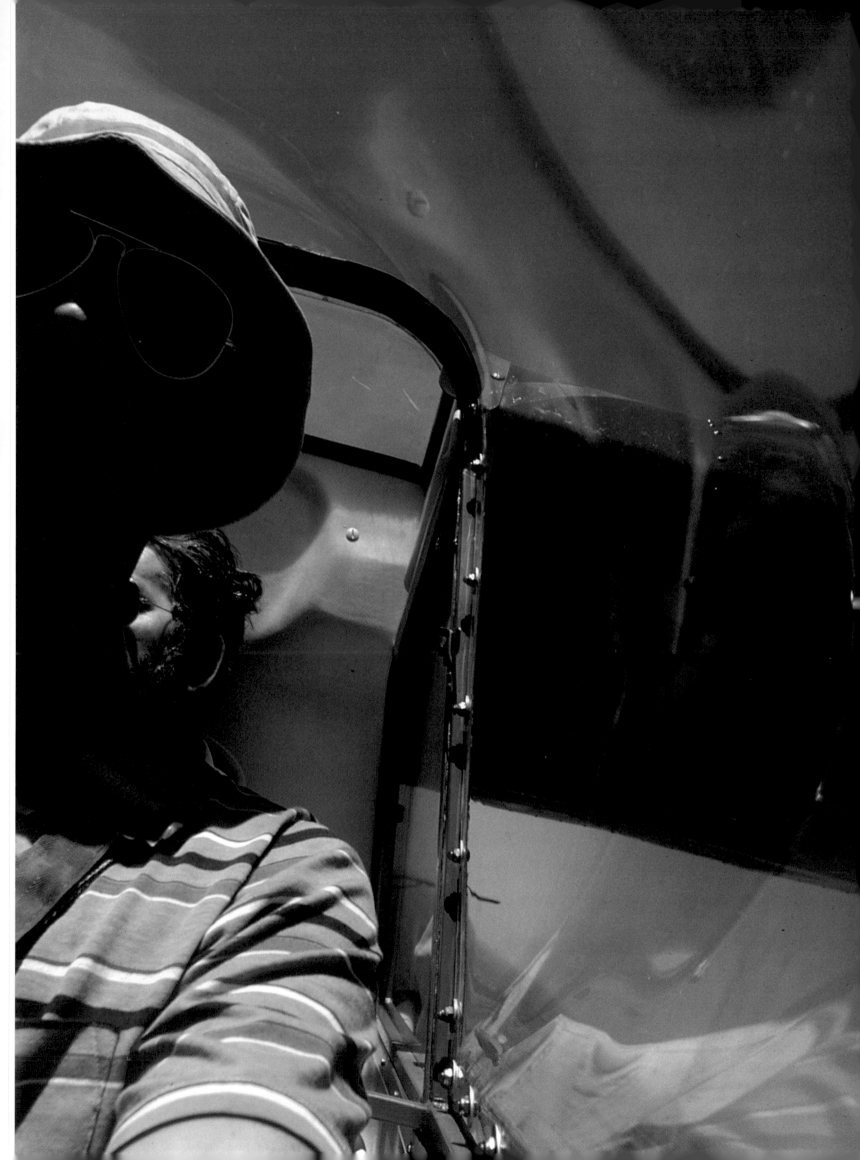

LUBBOCK'S FASCINATION WITH THE
sky stems from more than just agricultural concerns. During World
War II, the city was home to not
one, but two Army Air Corps bases.
And when there's an air show to be
seen, West Texans turn out in droves
to scan the skies.

FROM PERFORMANCES AT THE
*Lubbock Memorial Civic Center to
an Arts Festival rock concert, from
fiddlers to musicians gathered in
Buddy Holly Park for the annual
Tornado Jam, concerts abound
throughout the year in Lubbock.*

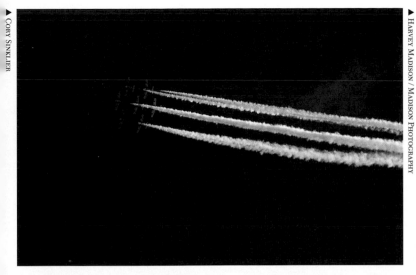

LUBBOCK'S FASCINATION WITH THE *sky stems from more than just agricultural concerns. During World War II, the city was home to not one, but two Army Air Corps bases. And when there's an air show to be seen, West Texans turn out in droves to scan the skies.*

WEST TEXANS LOVE THEIR RODEOS, *and Lubbock hosts two of them every year—the ABC Rodeo and Texas Tech's Intercollegiate Rodeo. Cowboys love the land, except when it comes rushing up to meet them as they fly off the back of a bull or bucking bronco.*

122

**IN ADDITION TO THE LAND, RODEO** *cowboys love rodeo clowns, and not for their entertainment value alone. When the cowboy clutches the reins, ready to come out of the chute, he knows the skillful clowns will be there at the end of a crucial ride, ready to distract the unruly animal and perhaps save the rider's life.*

PAGES 124 & 125:
SPECTATORS AT THE NATIONAL
Cowboy Symposium wait patiently
for the next event at the annual
gathering of working cowboy artists,
poets, and cooks, among others.

Cowboys from throughout the
country come together each fall for a
four-day weekend of auctions, arena
events, and entertainment.
PHOTO BY ASHTON THORNHILL

AS A FURTHER CELEBRATION OF the city's heritage, a group of Lubbock-area residents got together a few years ago to form a replica of the Fourth Cavalry Regiment of Col. Ronald MacKenzie, who traversed the area in the 1870s looking for Comanches. The regiment, complete with authentic uniforms and equipment, performs at local events and parades.

**THE RANCHING HERITAGE CENTER,** *adjacent to the Museum of Texas Tech University, serves as a living memorial to the development of ranching and the Wild West. Authentic furnishings and equipment mirror life in the early days of Texas, and 33 structures, such as the grand old ranch house (above), have been restored and moved to the site. The museum and Ranching Heritage Center are ideal hosts for the annual National Cowboy Symposium.*

WITH ALL THE AVAILABLE LAND, *Lubbock has naturally grown "out" instead of up, as new construction burgeons in every direction. Older additions such as the Rush area hold their own, while new additions march steadfastly toward the cotton fields surrounding the city.*

ANY WEST TEXAS CAT KNOWS *better than to mess with red-hot peppers, even if they're used as a decoration.*

EVERYTHING'S SUPPOSED TO BE
*bigger in Texas, but rest assured,
this is no house cat. Not far from
the city, Richard Wittenburg gives
one of his "pet" mountain lions a
big hug.*

LITTLE FOLKS LOVE LITTLE *critters, whether it's Lubbock's "Prairie Dog Pete" at Prairie Dog Town, or the traditional "bug in a jar."*

A NONPROFIT MUSEUM FOR SCIENCE education, the Science Spectrum provides quality demonstrations and hands-on exhibits for residents and visitors alike. The permanent and traveling exhibits are complemented by the Omnimax Theater, featuring an advanced motion picture system with a specially designed dome screen. The theater's 72 speakers are strategically placed in 10 clusters to allow six-track digital sound to move across the theater, synchronized with the action on the screen.

TWO CENTURIES AGO, THE IMMENSE
*canyon of yellowish earth that shel-
tered herds of buffalo, antelope,
mustangs, and wild longhorn cattle
was dubbed El Canyon de las Casas
Amarillas by Spanish explorers. Now
known as Yellowhouse Canyon, the
area once inhabited by Apaches and
the powerful Comanches serves as a
romantic reminder of Lubbock's past.*

CITY O

▲ Harvey Madison / Madison Photography

▲ Mark C. Mamawal

▲ Harvey Madison / Madison Photography

▲ Val Hildreth

**From any direction, visitors** *driving across the South Plains find an open door to a paradoxical combination of the old and new— yucca and sunflower crops and scores of different kinds of barbed wire surrounding plots of cultivated flowers.*

A PIONEER IN ABSTRACT NATURE *paintings, Georgia O'Keeffe must surely have been inspired by the stunning irises dotting the South Plains landscape. More than 500 varieties of the multihued beauties are grown in the Lubbock area.*

▲ VAL HILDRETH

AS HISTORIAN FRANCES HOLDEN has written, "If one defines culture as an expression of spirit, elevated by education and supported by good judgement, the Llano Estacado has presented its sons and daughters with a rare combination of nature, institutions, and heritage." Nature, indeed, has been good to this City of Land and Sky—but it's the people who have made it all come together.

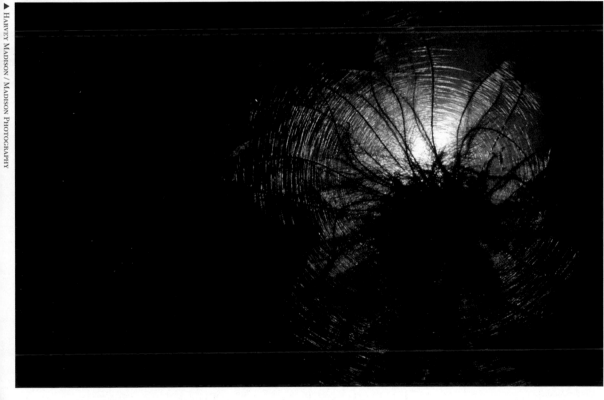

# EXCELLENCE

A LOOK AT THE CORPORATIONS,
BUSINESSES, PROFESSIONAL GROUPS, AND
COMMUNITY SERVICE ORGANIZATIONS
THAT HAVE MADE THIS BOOK POSSIBLE.

BY RICHARD & PENNY MASON

# 1900 - 1969

1901    FIRST NATIONAL BANK OF WEST TEXAS,
A NORWEST BANK

1907    LUBBOCK CHAMBER OF COMMERCE

1908    CRENSHAW, DUPREE & MILAM, L.L.P.

1908    JONES, FLYGARE, GALEY, BROWN & WHARTON

1909    CITY OF LUBBOCK

1917    LUBBOCK NATIONAL BANK

1918    LUBBOCK METHODIST HOSPITAL SYSTEM

1923    TEXAS TECH UNIVERSITY AND TEXAS TECH
UNIVERSITY HEALTH SCIENCES CENTER

1927    MCCLESKEY, HARRIGER, BRAZILL & GRAF, L.L.P.

1935    SANFORD INSURANCE AGENCY

1939    ST. MARY OF THE PLAINS HOSPITAL

1948    AMERICAN STATE BANK

1949    CARDIOLOGY ASSOCIATES OF LUBBOCK, P.A.

1955    UNITED SUPERMARKETS

1958    KLLL-FM

1960    FURR'S/BISHOP'S, INC.

1962    LUBBOCK ARTIFICIAL LIMB CO., INC.

1965    HIGHLAND MEDICAL CENTER

# FIRST NATIONAL BANK OF WEST TEXAS, A NORWEST BANK

THE SLOGAN "THE THINGS THAT LAST ALWAYS COME FIRST" IS AN APPROPRIATE ONE FOR FIRST NATIONAL BANK OF WEST TEXAS, THE SOUTH PLAINS' LARGEST FINANCIAL INSTITUTION. AS A CORPORATE CITIZEN AND A COMMUNITY BUSINESS LEADER, THE BANK HAS PLAYED

a key role in Lubbock's history since its organization in 1901 as the original Bank of Lubbock.

The bank was founded by L.A. Knight, Henry Slaton, O.L. Slaton, George C. Wolffarth, L.T. Lester,

HEADQUARTERED IN DOWNTOWN *Lubbock (right), First National was the first financial institution in Texas to locate a branch inside a Lubbock supermarket (above).*

Walter S. Posey, and Roy Riddel. Posey and Wolffarth both were members of Lubbock Townsite Company and later played key roles in developing Lubbock's charter when the city was incorporated in 1909. Their bank was recognized as First National Bank of Lubbock after the institution was issued a national charter in 1902. In January 1994, First National Bank merged with Norwest and is now known as First National Bank of West Texas, A Norwest Bank.

## SHAPING THE COMMUNITY

Terms such as dependability, quality service, and friendliness characterize First National Bank. As a full-service financial institution, the bank offers customers services such

as new accounts, CDs, IRAs, loans, trust services, safe-deposit boxes, and investments. Six branch locations and 17 automatic teller machines provide easy access for First National's customer base. The bank also operates the region's largest loan program for commercial enterprises, commodities, agriculture, individuals, and students. In fact, First National seeks to provide 100 percent of a customer's financial services and has achieved financial success by tailoring its products and

services to fit the needs of the community.

Despite significant growth over the years, banking remains a neighborly experience at First National. Staff members are friendly, attentive, and courteous, and reflect the bank's commitment to excellence and integrity. First National historically played a leadership role in the character of downtown Lubbock and was the first financial institution in Texas to locate branches on a university campus and inside a Lubbock supermarket.

The bank's tradition of leadership is evident in many ways. For example, First National had occupied its new high-rise headquarters for less than two years when the May 1970 tornado ripped through downtown Lubbock. Surrounded by destruction, the bank led the way in revitalizing the area as part of a surge of community spirit that has shaped modern Lubbock. Today, First National Bank makes the majority of loans in Lubbock and remains a responsible corporate citizen and business leader.

As cofounder Posey once remarked, whenever there was a job to be done in Lubbock, everybody pitched in and saw that it got done, whether that job was bringing in a railroad, building a new school, or founding a college. First National Bank's ongoing role as a community leader proves that Posey's sentiment is as alive today as it was more than 90 years ago.

# LUBBOCK NATIONAL BANK

L UBBOCK NATIONAL BANK IS PROUD OF ITS POSITION AS A LOCALLY OWNED, LOCALLY MANAGED COMMUNITY BANK. IN FACT, ITS PROACTIVE INVOLVEMENT IN CIVIC AFFAIRS EARNED IT ONE OF THE FIRST 60 "OUTSTANDING" RATINGS ISSUED NATIONALLY UNDER THE COMMUNITY

Reinvestment Act.

Complementing this focus on local needs is a commitment to fiscal stability. During recent years, Lubbock National's capital position has increased to one of the stron-

gest in Lubbock. The bank is well equipped to continue its mission of building a strong financial institution with quality customers by serving the needs of local citizens.

## SERVICE AND CONVENIENCE

Lubbock National Bank, with full-service locations on 50th and 82nd streets, has established itself as a leader in convenient, quality banking with an emphasis on individualized attention. For example, Lubbock National recently created PhoneBank. This service enables customers to monitor savings and checking accounts 24 hours a day and to transfer funds between accounts. PhoneBank lets customers conduct business over the telephone at any hour—regardless of the bank's schedule.

Lubbock National provides a variety of specialized services tailored to its diverse business clientele, including entrepreneurs, manufacturers, professionals, and executives. The bank also provides numerous investment services, such as annuities, mutual funds, and stocks and bonds. The investment staff can execute stock transactions or provide recommendations tailored to a customer's unique investment needs.

Lubbock National's longtime expertise in commercial lending to independent businesses was primarily responsible for its early growth. Today, the bank remains an active lender in areas ranging from consumer loans to specialized Small Business Administration packages. In 1991 Lubbock National acquired West Central Investment Corporation, a mortgage lender, and merged the company with its real estate department to meet customer needs for mortgages. Likewise, Lubbock National

offers interim lines of credit to help finance many new construction projects.

### INVESTING IN LUBBOCK

Lubbock National's heritage dates back to Lubbock's early days and to Charles Ernest Maedgen, Sr., a pioneer of the local banking indus-

try. In 1917 Maedgen founded what was to become Lubbock National Bank.

Through the decades, one thing has remained constant: the community orientation associated with Lubbock National. Investing more than just funds, the bank provides management expertise and financial assistance for many civic and charitable organizations. This community orientation, as applied to all aspects of its operations, will remain an important focus at Lubbock National. And, according to the bank's slogan, you can "Count on It!"

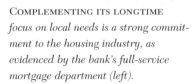

DAVID SEIM, PRESIDENT AND CEO OF *Lubbock National Bank.*

COMPLEMENTING ITS LONGTIME *focus on local needs is a strong commitment to the housing industry, as evidenced by the bank's full-service mortgage department (left).*

# CITY OF LUBBOCK

T HE STORY OF LUBBOCK'S CREATION IS CHARACTERISTIC OF THE COMMUNITY ITSELF. TWO RIVAL TOWNS VIED FOR RESIDENTS ON THE WEST TEXAS FRONTIER DURING THE 1890S UNTIL LEADERSHIP IN BOTH FLEDGLING SETTLEMENTS AGREED THAT SUCCESS DEPENDED UPON

MAXEY PARK AND FRANK HIGINBOTHAM *Park are among numerous recreational areas available to residents.*

LUBBOCK IS WIDELY KNOWN FOR *pleasant days capped by spectacular sunsets.*

cooperation. The towns combined to form a new community and, in an equitable solution to a common problem, awarded alternating lots by draw to members of the original rival towns.

That attitude of cooperation has been a community hallmark ever since. Whether it's winning a railroad through town in 1909, establishing Texas Tech University in 1923, building the Lubbock Army Airfield during World War II, or recovering from the May 1970 tornado that devastated the downtown area, Lubbock's people work together. Today, the city's population of more than 190,000 individuals is universally characterized as courteous and friendly. Nearly every week the local newspaper publishes a letter to the editor about a Good Samaritan who helped an out-of-town visitor overcome an unexpected problem. Those letters are evidence that

the Lubbock community is made of people—not houses, streets, or skyscrapers.

### SUPERB QUALITY OF LIFE

Lubbock's best-kept secret is the quality of life its residents enjoy. The city receives national recognition in surveys that target

quality of life, and cost-of-living indexes place Lubbock among the top 20 percent of communities nationwide for affordability. That means Lubbock residents live better at less cost, while enjoying access to a diverse range of housing, goods, and services found in larger urban areas, without the conges-

and Larry Wharton, for example, are active members of the American Board of Trial Advocates, the International Association of Defense Council, and the Texas Association of Defense Counsel.

Health care and hospital law is another area of practice for which the firm is well known. Charles Galey and John Flygare lead the firm in this rapidly evolving field of modern law. They represent health

care clients in medical malpractice, litigation, organizational and operational issues, managed care contracts, labor disputes, and other related legal issues.

Farming and ranching remains a vital part of Lubbock's economy. Harold P. "Bo" Brown, Jr., directs the firm's practice in agribusiness and banking law, representing local, regional, and international agribusiness clients in real estate

▲ VICTOR MOSQUEDA

ValuCare As
sors social a
throughout

**BRINGING**
**ENTIRE RE**
The Lubboc
System com
cal network
between Da

Affiliation a
pitals and re
300-mile rad
total license

tion and inconveniences.

The city's climate is characterized by sunshine on two of three days, and extended winter cold spells are rare. Summers rival anywhere in the world, with pleasant days capped by spectacular sunsets and cool nightly breezes.

Lubbock is the center for a diverse economy that blends agribusiness, medicine, education, and government. The city has a major military facility, Reese Air Force Base, and engages in regional wholesale and retail trade with communities across West Texas and eastern New Mexico. Lubbock agricultural and manufactured products reach all areas of the globe. And as Texas' wine industry continues to grow, several local vintners have received international recognition. The area also has a growing arts and entertainment community and was the home of rock-and-roll music legend Buddy Holly.

The city's population is remarkably young. Its median age is 29.3, four years younger than the national average. The workforce includes more than 113,000 individuals whose skills range from industrial assembly to law and medicine. The city is demographically diverse, with a population that is two-thirds Caucasian and one-third Hispanic, African-American, or other minority group. This blend contributes significantly to local leadership and the economy, while supplying the cultural diversity that keeps a community vibrant.

Seventy-eight percent of Lubbock's households are comprised of families, which explains a great deal about the city's quality of life.

## BUILDING ON A STRONG FOUNDATION
While Lubbock's people are its major asset, the community also has created a substantial infrastructure through a partnership between businesses, residents, and city government. Lubbock is serviced by an excellent transportation system, in-

cluding Interstate 27, which places the rapidly growing southwest corridor of the city within 10 minutes of downtown. A second crosstown freeway will be constructed by decade's end.

Lubbock traditionally has been called the "Hub City" because railroads and state and federal highways converge on the community. Lubbock International Airport offers more than 40 daily arrivals and departures for an estimated half-million passengers annually in a modern, 22,000-square-foot terminal with convenient access.

The city is served by two electric utilities, including municipally owned Lubbock Power & Light. LP&L proceeds offset portions of the city's operating budget and reduce local property taxes, while ensuring some of the lowest electric rates through competition.

With a student population of 34,000 in two major school districts, low student/teacher ratios, and high graduation rates, Lubbock students are well educated. The city furnished five of 13 Texas teams that advanced to the international finals in the Odyssey of the Mind competition, and one of the city's high schools won the National Science Bowl competition for two consecutive years. Four universities, including Texas Tech with its seven colleges and professional schools in law and medicine, round out the educational picture. Lub-

bock also serves as the medical center for the entire West Texas and eastern New Mexico region and offers the most diversified health care services between Dallas and Phoenix.

A diverse complement of museums entertain visitors and residents alike with a variety of interests. The inquisitive can study Stone Age North America at the internationally recognized Lubbock Lake Landmark State Historical Park, the historic American West at the Ranching Heritage Center, or cutting-edge technology at the Science Spectrum and the Omnimax theater.

In recent years, the city has undergone a renewal in spirit. A new mayor and city council have taken a leadership role in nurturing the local partnership between business and government while developing relationships with smaller communities on the South Plains to promote mutual economic interests. For example, when Lubbock entered a competition in 1993 to gain a federal accounting installation, residents overwhelmingly backed an increase in local taxes to pay for the incentive package. When the competition was scrapped at the federal level, the city's elected leaders spearheaded the drive to repeal the tax. That spirit of local cooperation plays a key role in developing and maintaining the quality of life Lubbock residents enjoy.

THE AREA BOASTS A DIVERSE, STABLE *economy that blends agribusiness, oil, higher education, and health care (above). Lubbock was home to rock-and-roll music legend Buddy Holly (below).*

## JONES, FLYGARE, GA[...]

**A**S THE OLDEST LAW [...]
& WHARTON VALU[...]
THE FIRM'S FOUN[...]
ATTRACTED BY T[...]

found instead a rapidly developing pioneer community in need of many services. Bean became a justice of the peace and, in 1901, was licensed to practice law. When the Santa Fe Railroad established a depot in Lubbock, other lawyers immigrated to the growing community, including E.L. Klett.

In 1908 Bean formed a law partnership with Klett, marking the formal beginning of the present-day firm. Although Bean and Klett dissolved their partnership in 1934, they continued to keep offices next to each other and provide mutual assistance when needed. Bean was joined in practice that year by his son, Robert, and by William H "Bill" Evans in 1937. Evans serve[...] as a board member for the Lubbo[...] Independent School District and the Texas State Board of Education. Evans Junior High School i[...] Lubbock is named in his honor.

*MEMBERS OF THE FIRM INCLUDE (seated, from left) Myrtle McDonald, Michael Reed, John LeVick, (standing, from left) John Rosentreter, Brad Pettiet, Lois Wischkaemper, and Jeff Jones.*

JOY VISUAL PRODUCTIONS

METHOD[...]
is the regi[...]
dedicated[...]
of childre[...]
is evident[...]
ment that[...]
children c[...]

## HIGHLAND MEDICAL CENTER

**F**OR THREE DECADES, HIGHLAND MEDICAL CENTER HAS HONED ITS FOCUS ON THE HEALTH CARE NEEDS OF FAMILIES IN WEST TEXAS. THE MEDICAL COMPLEX, CONVENIENTLY LOCATED AT 50TH STREET AND UNIVERSITY AVENUE IN LUBBOCK, PROVIDES MORE THAN 25 SERVICES IN A SETTING designed to meet the personal needs of individual patients.

Licensed for 123 beds, Highland delivers quality health care in a modern setting. The medical center, with staff privileges for 150 physicians, provides access to family practitioners, internists, and general practice physicians, as well as pediatrics, obstetrics/gynecology services, and a wide array of other specialists.

### GROWING TO MEET THE NEEDS OF WEST TEXANS

Highland Medical Center's growth continued after Houston-based Community Health Systems, Inc. bought the hospital in 1986. Following a major renovation of the existing facilities, several programs were added to further meet the needs of Lubbock families. Today, Highland is one of 20 facilities in the United States owned by Community Health Systems, which continues to invest in the hospital and the community.

Recently, Community Health Systems signed an agreement to merge with Hallmark Healthcare Corporation, which will nearly double the number of hospitals owned and operated by the company. Under the merger, Community Health will expand to 38 hospitals in 16 states, representing more than 6,500 employees, 3,000 physicians, and 3,044 licensed hospital beds.

Highland has taken an active role in promoting healthier lifestyles through a community education speakers bureau and by hosting educational seminars on prevention for the general public.

The medical center also sponsors the Highland Regional Center for Diabetes, a comprehensive program for diabetes treatment. Effectively combining education, counseling, and monitoring, the program's team approach brings together a medical director, registered dietitian, exercise physiologist, pharmacist, psychological consultant, and podiatrist. At the center of the program is Living Well with Diabetes, a

*HIGHLAND MEDICAL CENTER, conveniently located at 50th Street and University Avenue in Lubbock, delivers quality health care in a modern setting.*

In 1989 the hospital expanded its services by entering a joint venture with Lubbock physicians to construct the Highland Imaging Center, a high-tech diagnostic facility that features a $1.2 million CT scanner.

But what sets Highland apart is the progressive vision expressed in its motto: "Your Family's Health Begins Here."

three-week course aimed at helping people with diabetes lead active lives.

## PERSONAL ATTENTION FOR PATIENTS AND THEIR FAMILIES

Highland's size fosters an atmosphere in which employees get to know their coworkers—whether they are administrators, doctors, support staff, or lab technicians. In turn, the hospital extends this friendly, caring attitude to its patients, providing them with special attention rarely found in larger facilities.

To further enhance this commitment to active listening, the hospital has developed a program through which each patient is assigned an "ambassador" to address individual expectations and needs. Should a problem arise, the ambassador becomes a resource for solving the problem immediately.

In addition to acute care, the hospital's 12-bed skilled nursing unit provides one-on-one specialized services for patients who do not require intensive care or a surgical bed but who are too sick to return to their residence, retirement community, or nursing home. The unit also gives personal attention to transition patients on their way to physical rehabilitation.

Highland Medical Center is fully equipped for outpatient diagnostic procedures, including lab, X-ray, ultrasound, mammography, and magnetic resonance imaging. Highland also houses an endoscopy lab for the purpose of diagnosing diseases of the digestive system.

Most important to Highland is its commitment to family health care. The facility recently added a birthing center, The Baby Place, which offers a warm, comfortable atmosphere, as well as highly trained nurses and doctors to assure excellent delivery care. Special amenities include birthing classes, infant CPR instruction, and dinner for two before the parents leave for home.

At Highland, the patients decide who visits them and how many

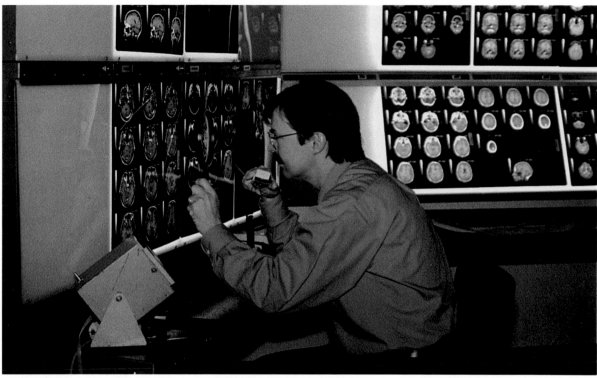

visitors they wish to have. Family members and friends of patients are always welcome at Highland, because of the important role they play in the delivery of health care and the road to recovery.

This approach is evident at the 14-bed Highland Family Rehabilitation Center where family members take part in therapeutic sessions designed to help individuals return to their daily routine after a catastrophic illness or injury. Similarly, the staff at Highland's

skilled nursing unit provides training for families through education and after-care planning and assistance.

For nearly 30 years, Highland Medical Center has delivered modern medical care while remaining sensitive to the needs of individual patients and their families. As it enters a new decade of service, the hospital looks forward to addressing the changing health care environment in Lubbock and surrounding communities.

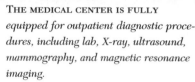

THE MEDICAL CENTER IS FULLY *equipped for outpatient diagnostic procedures, including lab, X-ray, ultrasound, mammography, and magnetic resonance imaging.*

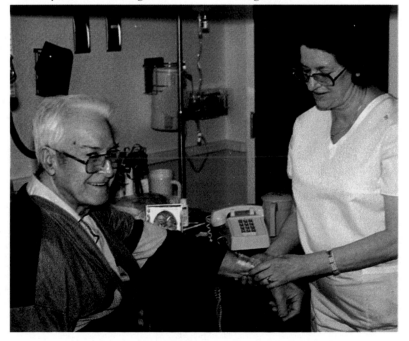

THE HOSPITAL STAFF EXTENDS A *friendly, caring attitude to its patients, providing them with special attention rarely found in larger facilities.*

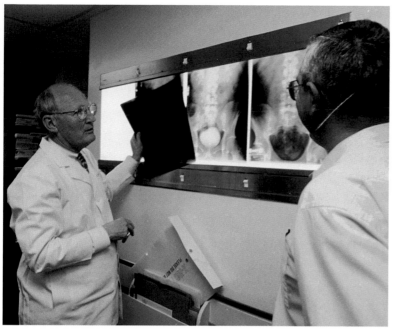

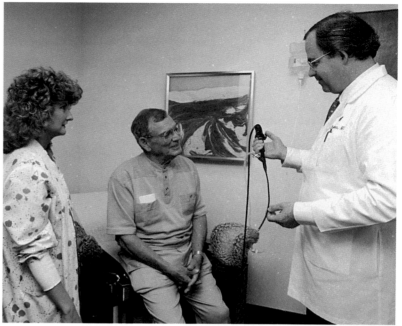

## A LONG-STANDING COMMITMENT TO SERVING WEST TEXANS

Stalcup has had a lifelong fascination with Lubbock. His father was employed in the petroleum industry for Halliburton Company, an oil field services firm, and the family lived in several West Texas towns. Stalcup attended elementary school in Monahans, junior high school in Kermit and Levelland, and high school in Midland. He then attended the Massachusetts Institute of Technology in Cambridge and the University of Texas Medical School in Galveston.

Stalcup chose Lubbock as the site to begin permanent practice in 1971, a time when most physicians had ceased making home visits. However, he envisioned bringing modern medical care to the people of rural West Texas and began biweekly visits to the communities of Matador and Floydada on the Texas South Plains. Floydada Community Hospital provided him use of its emergency room. In the ranching community of Matador, the hospital board leased a previously closed community hospital to Stalcup for a monthly fee of $28. Stalcup hired Jean Cooper as nurse and local liaison.

Additional expertise and an international flair were added to the practice when Brothers joined Stal-

cup in 1986 after working for the American British Hospital in Mexico City. Brothers trained in Mexico City for the first four years of his medical education, continued his surgery education in Louisville, and completed his urology training at Tulane University in New Orleans. Brothers is fluent in both Spanish and English and chose Lubbock as a site to enter medical practice because of its reputation as a leading medical center and the quality of life the community offered.

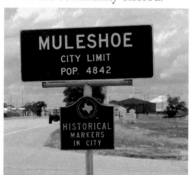

When Brothers joined the practice, Lubbock Urology Associates opened another clinic in Levelland in an effort to continue the tradition of service to rural communities. He shares Stalcup's appreciation for the friendliness of rural West Texas. "People outside the city are different," Brothers says. "They are more relaxed and appreciative. It is the highlight of my week to go see the good folks of Levelland." Stalcup and

Brothers have plans to open a similar clinic in Muleshoe, 90 miles outside of Lubbock.

In 1988 LUA was involved in a pilot partnership program offered to Reese Air Force Base personnel and military retirees in Lubbock. The program is unique in that civilian medical doctors become partners with military doctors to provide active and retired military personnel with health care. The program has now become a model for other military bases across the

United States and continues today.

With its longtime commitment to quality and personalized urological care for the people of West Texas, it is clear that Lubbock Urology Associates is redefining the doctor-patient relationship on the Texas South Plains.

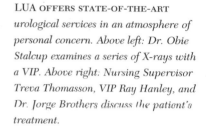

LUA OFFERS STATE-OF-THE-ART *urological services in an atmosphere of personal concern. Above left: Dr. Obie Stalcup examines a series of X-rays with a VIP. Above right: Nursing Supervisor Treva Thomasson, VIP Ray Hanley, and Dr. Jorge Brothers discuss the patient's treatment.*

LUBBOCK UROLOGY ASSOCIATES *currently operates a clinic in Levelland and plans to open another in Muleshoe. Since 1988 LUA has participated in a partnership program offered to Reese Air Force Base personnel and military retirees in Lubbock.*

# COX CABLE LUBBOCK, INC.

**F**OR 24 YEARS, COX CABLE LUBBOCK, INC. HAS PROVIDED LOCAL SUB-
SCRIBERS "QUALITY YOU CAN COUNT ON" WHEN IT COMES TO CABLE
TELEVISION. THE COMPANY SERVICES OVER 43,000 CUSTOMERS THROUGH
656 MILES OF CABLE WITH A SUBSCRIPTION SERVICE THAT PROVIDES A

choice of basic cable television packages, six premium options, and four pay-per-view channels. The company also offers Music Choice, formerly Digital Cable Radio, a commercial-free audio service featuring 30 channels of digital quality sound.

## MAKING A DIFFERENCE IN LUBBOCK
Cox Cable has a positive impact on the Lubbock economy. The company employs 135 people locally with an annual payroll of $2.9 million and is one of 24 cable systems operated in the United States by Cox Cable Communications, a division of Atlanta-based Cox Enterprises, Inc. In 1993 the company paid over $483,000

scores a commitment to the community that has attracted cable industry recognition, including awards in three of four categories from the Texas Cable Television Association for leadership in developing programs that benefit the community. Cox Cable received one of only two Gold Awards in Texas for the company's hour-long program, "Students' View '92: The Presidency." The program also received the Innovator Award for Community Service from *CableVision* magazine in October of 1993.

Cox Cable annually donates more than $55,000 in airtime and production to help nonprofit organizations get their message out to the Lubbock community; it has pro-

Cable was joined by 100 other local teams in raising $115,000 for the March of Dimes fight against birth defects in 1994.

## UPGRADING FOR THE FUTURE
The company undertook a massive remodeling program in September 1993 to upgrade its facilities to accommodate the rapidly evolving television technology—known as the information superhighway—and to provide a pleasant customer service environment. The upgrade is part of a continuing emphasis on quality customer service. Training programs emphasize answering a customer's question on the first call, and the company utilizes an Automated Response Unit to allow customers to check account bal-

COX CABLE STRIVES TO BE A LEADER *in today's rapidly evolving technology.*

*EXTENSIVE REMODELING WAS COM-
pleted in August of 1994, in part to
provide a more pleasant customer service
area that deals with approximately 8,500
people each month.*

COX CABLE SUPPORTS LISD-TV CABLE *channel 12 by providing educational access channels and assisting the Lubbock Independent School District in establishing interactive classrooms.*

in franchise fees to the City of Lubbock, contributed property taxes of nearly $300,000, and spent $1.6 million with local businesses at an estimated economic impact of $15.5 million.

The company's high level of service involves more than dollars, however. Cox Cable's slogan, "Proud to Be Lubbock," under-

vided more than $43,000 in materials and services to the Lubbock Independent School District. The company continues to support LISD-TV Channel 12 by providing educational access channels and assisting the school district in establishing interactive television in the classroom. As corporate sponsor of March of Dimes WalkAmerica, Cox

ances after hours or initiate repairs in the event of a lost cable signal.

These continuing upgrades are part of Cox Cable's long-term plans to build on the solid foundation it has established through 24 years of service to the Lubbock community.

# SOUTH PLAINS MALL

**T**HERE'S ALWAYS SOMETHING NEW AT SOUTH PLAINS MALL. AS THE LARGEST SHOPPING CENTER IN WEST TEXAS, THE MALL OFFERS RETAIL CHOICES THAT RANGE FROM FASHION AND FOOD TO GIFTS, ELECTRON-ICS, FINE JEWELRY, ATHLETIC SUPPLIES, AND MORE IN FIVE MAJOR

department stores and 150 specialty shops.

Strategically located at the intersection of South Loop 289 and Slide Road, South Plains Mall is within a 15-minute drive of 95 percent of the city's population. The southwest Lubbock location also makes the mall a convenient destination for out-of-town visitors.

## THE PLACE TO SHOP IN LUBBOCK

South Plains Mall is a natural magnet for shoppers. The mall also serves as a convenient stop for hairstyling, optical services, boot and shoe repair, and photofinishing. Familiar anchor stores—Dillard's, JCPenney, Sears, Mervyn's, and Bealls—operate among the many smaller retail outlets that include The Gap, Eddie Bauer, Victoria's Secret, Bombay Company, Wet Seal, and The Disney Store. Attractive fountains add sparkle to the indoor ambience, while alcoves of trees and benches provide convenient rest areas for shoppers. In any given week, the mall draws an estimated 200,000 people to its enclosed, climate-controlled environment.

In recent years, many individuals have come to South Plains Mall to enjoy a safe, weather-free environment for exercise and fitness. The facility is open to walkers Monday through Saturday at 6:00 a.m. through the main entrance, and the mall's walker organization, the Heart and Sole Club, meets monthly.

## HISTORY-MAKING GROWTH

C & A Investment Co. of Scottsdale, Arizona, constructed the retail facility in the midst of a building boom that followed the 1970 Lubbock tornado. At that time, the mall represented the largest construc-

tion permit ever issued by the City of Lubbock Building Inspection Department. The original $10 million permit was the first in a series of initial expenditures that totaled $25 million. When the facility

opened its doors in July 1972, South Plains Mall housed 48 stores in 854,664 square feet of enclosed space and became the largest single taxpayer in Lubbock County.

Since then, the facility has undergone expansion at regular intervals and currently comprises more than 150 stores in 1.3 million square feet of space, comparing favorably to retail centers in major metropolitan areas. Paramount Group Inc. of New York purchased the mall in 1981 and continues to operate the facility.

Over the years, South Plains Mall has had a dramatic impact on the region's shopping habits. In fact, when it opened, the facility expanded Lubbock's retail trade territory to include West Texas and eastern New Mexico. While downtown Lubbock has evolved into a center for business, legal services, and government, most of the city's retail development has taken place

in the mall's vicinity. Thanks to the vibrant growth of Lubbock and the loyalty of its West Texas shoppers, South Plains Mall continues to thrive and serve the area's one-stop shopping needs.

SHOPPERS OF ALL AGES ENJOY RETAIL *choices that range from fashion and food to gifts, electronics, fine jewelry, and athletic supplies. In any given week, the mall draws an estimated 200,000 people to its enclosed, climate-controlled environment.*

215

# SOUTH PARK HOSPITAL

OUTH PARK HOSPITAL HAS DEVELOPED ITS OWN PROGRAM FOR HEALTH CARE REFORM. THE 99-BED FACILITY, THE ONLY FULL-SERVICE HOSPITAL IN LUBBOCK'S HEAVILY POPULATED SOUTHWEST CORRIDOR, PLACES A STRONG EMPHASIS ON CUSTOMER SERVICE. "OUR STRENGTH IS OUR SIZE," EXPLAINS

Steve Rowley, South Park's chief executive officer. "Because we are a small hospital, we are able to concentrate on the quality of care we offer our patients."

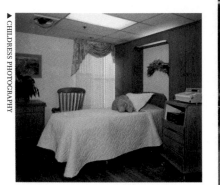

EVERY DAY IS "MOTHER'S DAY" AT *the Women's Custom Care Center, which includes attractive, comfortably appointed labor, delivery, and recovery rooms.*

South Park does so through a program titled Custom Care. Because no two patients are alike, treatment plans are specially designed to meet the unique needs of South Park patients. "We like to take the time to get to know our patients as people, not as case or room numbers," Rowley says.

The medical facility offers the residents of Lubbock and surrounding communities the highest quality medical care while maintaining low costs. With its convenient location at the corner of Quaker Avenue and South Loop 289, the hospital is easily accessible to patients from throughout the area.

### CUSTOMER SERVICE IN ACTION
Originally built in 1974, South Park Hospital was purchased in 1984 by Summit Health, Ltd. of Burbank, California. Then, in 1994 Summit joined with Nashville, Tennessee-based OrNda Healthcare to create

A HOMELIKE ENVIRONMENT PREVAILS *in the beautifully furnished rooms of South Park's Custom Care Surgicenter.*

the fifth-largest hospital chain in the United States. South Park's partnership with the chain provides cost advantages that complement its ongoing commitment to customer service. In May 1994, South Park and Methodist Hospital announced an affiliation agreement that provides an ongoing relationship of support, sharing of technology, joint continuing education, and development of a managed care product.

This hospitalwide emphasis on service is a strong selling point on the Texas South Plains, where people prefer the friendliness of interpersonal relationships, even when it includes a trip to the hospital. South Park has the advantage of being large enough to provide quality health care from a staff of highly trained physicians and support staff while being the right size to remember each patient's name. The hospital also is fully accredited by the Joint Commission on Accreditation of Healthcare Organizations.

South Park's focus on service is evident as soon as a patient enters the hospital. Rooms overlook garden atriums, a local lake,

or the attractively landscaped grounds surrounding the hospital campus. First-floor rooms even have sliding doors that open onto a patiolike area.

The hospital also has updated each patient room with furnishings that provide a homelike setting in which to receive medical care. Instead of the sterile environment that characterizes many other health care facilities, patients at South Park experience a nurturing atmosphere that complements the healing process. In fact, the hospital staff thinks of its customers as guests rather than patients.

### DIVERSE MEDICAL EXPERTISE
South Park Hospital has several areas of medical expertise, with an emphasis on emergency care, obstetrics, and outpatient surgery/ services.

The 24-hour emergency room, for example, is the only one in the Lubbock area to provide patients a 20-minute guarantee. Simply stated, the hospital promises that if a patient does not see an emergency room physician within 20 minutes of arrival, he or she will not be billed for the services. While studies show most emergency room waits exceed an hour, South Park Hospital continues to meet the 20-minute guarantee despite rapidly growing demand.

More recent developments at the hospital include the newly remodeled obstetrics unit, a state-of-the-art facility with large, comfortably appointed labor, delivery, and recovery rooms complete with computerized monitoring systems, a surgical suite for cesarean sections, and postpartum rooms that provide new parents the warmth and comfort of a homelike environment. The obstetrics unit overlooks two tropical atriums and offers

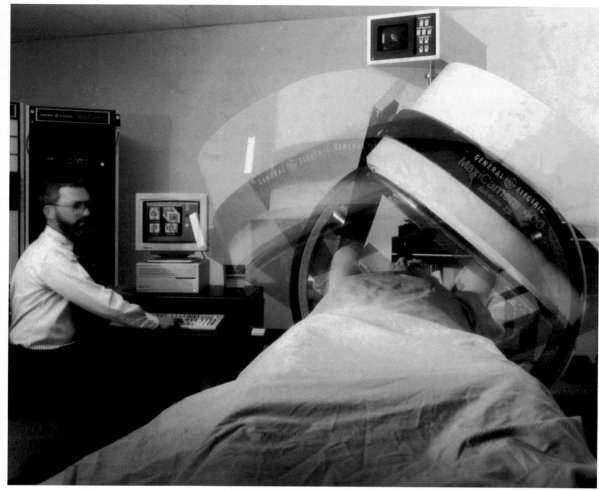

couples a candlelight dinner to celebrate the arrival of their newest family member.

In 1992 South Park Hospital established the Childbirth Network, a communitywide service that provides free pregnancy testing, educational information, and physician referral for women. The network operates two Lubbock locations for easy access.

Among the hospital's outpatient services is the Pain Medicine Clinic located on the hospital campus. The full-service clinic, which addresses chronic pain and associated problems, is under the direction of a board-certified anesthesiologist/pain medicine specialist who is available for consultations as well as referrals for pain relief measures. Typical treatments include medication, physical therapy, injections, or implants for patients suffering chronic pain.

In addition, South Park operates the 20-bed Custom Care Surgicenter, an outpatient facility

complete with private rooms and centralized scheduling for physicians. Among the many services available at the Custom Care Surgicenter are endoscopic procedures, hernia repair, gynecological surgery, arthroscopy, and ear-nose-throat procedures.

The hospital's outpatient services also encompass a custom rehabilitation center featuring technically advanced diagnostic and rehabilitation facilities that offer isokinetic testing equipment and physical therapy. The rehabilitation center provides sports and industrial screenings, seminars, and physical exams to complement regular treatment schedules. The center also operates a complete fitness center for Lubbock residents.

One of the hospital's most distinctive services is Lite Life, a surgical weight loss program for persons who are 100 or more pounds overweight. Geared toward individuals whose lives are endangered by conditions associated

with obesity, Lite Life attracts patients to Lubbock from across the United States. The program combines professional counseling and behavioral modification techniques and has been endorsed by the National Institutes of Health.

SOUTH PARK'S RENOVATED EMERGENCY *Services Department offers the area's only 20-minute guarantee.*

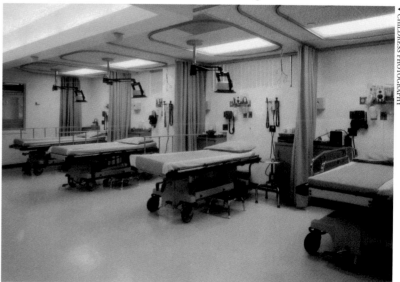

# EAGLE-PICHER INDUSTRIES
## CONSTRUCTION EQUIPMENT DIVISION

THE CONSTRUCTION EQUIPMENT DIVISION OF EAGLE-PICHER INDUSTRIES (EPI-CED) BUILDS PRODUCTS IN LUBBOCK THAT TOUCH THE FAR CORNERS OF THE GLOBE. THE HEAVY EARTHMOVERS AND FORKLIFT TRUCKS, MANUFACTURED AT THE PLANT UNDER AN EXCLUSIVE CONTRACT

EPI-CED IS PROUD OF ITS WEST TEXAS *heritage, which dates back to its predecessor's founding in 1927.*

for Caterpillar, Inc., are working in many countries around the world.

The Lubbock plant of EPI-CED is the sole manufacturer of elevating wheel tractor scrapers for Caterpillar and certain forklift trucks used in worldwide construction and other industrial applications. This significant achievement builds on a combination of West Texas work ethic, advanced manufacturing techniques, and total commitment to quality.

EPI-CED, located at 1802 East 50th Street in Lubbock, employs almost 700 people. These include highly skilled machinists, welders, assemblers, painters, engineers, buyers, and other production support personnel. The company's employees come not only from Lubbock but also from Plainview, Post, Littlefield, and other surrounding towns. As home to Texas Tech University and several community colleges and technical trade schools, Lubbock provides the broad base of skills EPI-CED

needs to compete globally. In addition, the city's affordable cost of living, low cost of doing business, and strong family values give EPI-CED and its employees an attractive place to work and live.

EPI-CED has three primary product lines. First, the company develops and manufactures elevating wheel tractor scrapers. These are large, self-propelled earthmoving machines used in road building and other heavy construction applications. Next, EPI-CED designs and manufactures two types of forklift trucks, which are marketed under the Caterpillar name. These units move materials in industrial and rough terrain applications. The company also manufactures a line of forklift trucks for Mitsubishi Caterpillar Forklift America (MCFA). Last, EPI-CED works as a subcontractor for Stewart & Stevenson to produce parts for the Family of Medium Tactical Vehicles (FMTV) for the Department of Defense.

### A TRADITION OF INNOVATION
The year 1927 marked the beginning of EPI-CED, when the Welderz Frend Generator Company was established in Amarillo to manufacture acetylene generators. In 1945 R.C. Johnson bought the company, moved it to Lubbock, and changed its name to Johnson Manufacturing Company. The company moved into a new plant in 1947. In that location, Johnson Manufacturing used its welding expertise to develop a line of farm implements, including cotton strippers, planters, rotary hoes, and stalk cutters.

In 1956 elevating scrapers were added to the company's product line, employing technology that is still in use today. A wheeled tractor pulls the scraper, and hydraulics adjust the scraper's bowl height above the ground and operate the elevating scraper system. The scraper shaves the ground's surface and transports dirt up and into the bowl by means of an elevator. Once

AMONG THE COMPANY'S NEARLY 700 *employees are many of Lubbock's welders, as well as machinists, assemblers, painters, engineers, buyers, and other production support personnel.*

THE VERTICAL TURRET LATHE IS PART *of a world-class manufacturing cell.*

THE EPI-CED PLANT AND TEST TRACK *are situated on 69 acres in Lubbock (left).*

the bowl is full, the tractor carries the dirt away for dumping. Johnson Manufacturing Company developed several patented techniques for this process, including the hydraulics that make the elevating scraper one of the most successful and efficient pieces of equipment for road construction and site preparation. Jim Lowder, who later served as division president, created several innovations in elevating scrapers. Initially, International Harvester, John Deere, and Caterpillar bought these units.

In 1964 Johnson Manufacturing moved into a larger plant at the company's present location. Simultaneously, it negotiated an exclusive contract with Caterpillar Tractor Company (now Caterpillar, Inc.) to manufacture 21-cubic-yard elevating scrapers. Today, EPI-CED produces four different sizes of elevating scrapers with capacities of 11, 16, 23, and 34 cubic yards of material. Caterpillar markets these machines under its trade name throughout the world.

In 1973 Eagle-Picher Industries of Cincinnati purchased Johnson Manufacturing Company and operates it now as the Construction Equipment Division. The division's two plants are among the more than 50 Eagle-Picher facilities

WHEEL TRACTOR SCRAPERS ARE USED *in various applications, such as highway/ heavy construction, building contracting, site development, mining, and material production (left). EPI-CED forklifts are marketed worldwide under the Caterpillar name (top). The Johnson 5-cubic-yard scraper is a forerunner of those manufactured at EPI-CED today (bottom).*

# KJTV34

On December 11, 1981, a bitter cold day in Lubbock, KJTV34 signed on with the John Wayne classic *Rio Lobo*. The signal was sent from an unheated trailer backed up to a transmitter in the middle of a cotton field. ■ "The more I learned about this business, the more I was convinced that my dad was crazy to go into television when and where he did," recalls General Manager Brad Moran, son of the station's founder Ray Moran. The idea of kicking off an independent television station in a small market already dominated by three established affiliates had many West Texans doubting KJTV34's ability to survive.

"But now Ray has proved me and many other people wrong," says Brad. Despite the unlikely beginning, KJTV34 today broadcasts from a $2.6 million, 12,000-square-foot, state-of-the-art facility and is a nationally recognized model of success for Fox television stations that compete in markets against the "three old networks."

KJTV34 is owned by Ray, his wife Mary, and Brad Moran through Lubbock-based Ramar

KJTV34 is owned by (from left) *Brad, Mary, and Ray Moran through Lubbock-based Ramar Communications.*

Communications. The company originally entered the local broadcasting market by building KTEZ radio in 1973, the first stand-alone FM station in Lubbock. The Morans sold KTEZ in 1983 and later purchased Spanish-language stations KXTQ-AM and KXTQ-FM in 1993 (subject to FCC approval). The radio stations are now known as Magic 93 and broadcast the very popular Tejano music format. The company also started the local Telemundo affiliate, a Spanish-language television station, which broadcasts on channel 46.

Ramar Communications is best known, however, for KJTV34, its flagship television station, which broadcasts on channel 34. The Morans ventured into television broadcasting in a roundabout way. Ray had acquired an FCC radio license in 1979 and, while negotiating rent for antenna space, suddenly found himself the owner of an 893-foot television tower south of Lubbock. Ray competed for and won an FCC television license for channel 34 in 1981 and, by year-end, had acquired a used mobile production truck with which to begin television broadcasts.

The biggest step in KJTV34's growth occurred in April 1987, when Fox Television Network developed a prime-time schedule well suited to independent television stations like KJTV34.

The station was the number one independent in the state of Texas by the time Fox began prime-time programming. "We had achieved a certain level of success when Fox came along, but to take things to the next level, we needed to be part of a larger group," Brad recalls. "That was the same story in markets all around the country, and that's why there are now 145 Fox stations."

Today, the station consistently ranks among the top 10 Fox stations in the nation and has a greater share of local audience than any other Fox station in Texas.

In November 1992, the Fox network had only 15 stations that were number one within their market during prime time. KJTV34 was one of those stations. Now that Fox has purchased the rights to telecast National Football Conference games—including the regionally idolized Dallas Cowboys—KJTV34 is poised to be the major player in the Lubbock television market.

The station has a knack for creating value. First it was through programming that viewers wanted to watch. Then Ray approached commercial television production in Lubbock as a high-quality service for his customers. The company purchased quality equipment and hired the skilled people who knew how to make it work. Today, informal surveys show the station has gained more than half of Lubbock's agency-generated commercial production market.

"Edit One" is the nerve center *of KJTV's $2.6 million facility.*

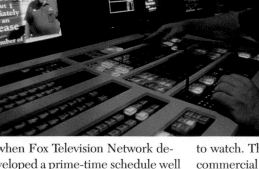

THE FOX34 KIDSCLUB HAS OVER 25,000 *members ranging in age from two to 14.*

KJTV's LUBBOCK FACILITY INCLUDES *an in-house fitness room.*

"We designed this building in 1986 as a postproduction facility," Ray says. "We created an environment where the client is taken care of with great people and with state-of-the-art equipment. At our station, clients are our top priority, as opposed to the news."

KJTV34 has established expanded coverage in outlying communities with translators and

graduates of Texas Tech and provides good benefits and training. Such success does not go unnoticed. KJTV34 alumni are now found in leadership positions in major television markets such as Los Angeles, Chicago, and Portland, Oregon.

As a locally owned station, KJTV34 strives to be a good corporate citizen. The station is involved

program is telecast before most holidays to discourage drinking and driving.

With plans to expand the Lubbock facility to accommodate broadcasting space for the company's radio stations and an eye on starting another independent television station in Albuquerque, Ramar Communications is poised to provide services for a growing

MAGIC 93's STATE-OF-THE-ART DIGITAL *control room (far left).*

THE EMPLOYEES OF RAMAR COMMUNI-*cations—including KJTV, Telemundo, and Magic 93—are proud of the organization's many awards in promotion and production (near left).*

carriage on cable systems in West Texas and eastern New Mexico that increase the station's geographic reach and provide greater access to viewers for advertisers. Ramar currently employs 55 people in Lubbock between the radio and television stations. The company also owns a radio station in Albuquerque, New Mexico. In Lubbock, KJTV34 frequently hires

in several civic endeavors, providing numerous volunteers each year. KJTV34 also produces United Way's annual video and is a leader in local contributions. The station regularly creates long-form videos for various public service projects in Lubbock, such as a 30-minute DWI Awareness program for the regional Emergency Medical Service ambulance system. That

number of viewers and the advertisers who want to reach them.

The Morans' roots are in Lubbock, and that is why Ray and Mary chose to pursue a television career here. Brad agrees: "We've been a success story because the people of Lubbock have watched and enjoyed what we've done—and we're a product of our viewership."

# Pat Ham, Inc., REALTORS

**E**VERYTHING PAT HAM, INC., REALTORS TOUCHES TURNS TO "SOLD." THE COMPANY'S 19 ENERGETIC REAL ESTATE AGENTS USE THEIR MAGIC TOUCH TO MAKE THE FIRM ONE OF LUBBOCK'S LEADING REAL ESTATE BUSI-NESSES. ■ LEADING THE WAY IS THE COMPANY'S OWNER AND PRESIDENT,

PAT HAM, THE COMPANY'S OWNER *and president, has been Lubbock's "Top Producer" since 1980.*

Pat Ham, a Lubbock native who has been the city's "Top Producer" since 1980. After discovering her special skills at generating sales, Pat decided to start her own company in the fall of 1984. In January 1985, she and Beverley Albin, the firm's first principal broker and sales manager, moved with a small support staff into the current offices on Quaker Avenue, south of the Loop.

At the time, Pat Ham, Inc., REAL-TORS occupied the only structure between the Loop and 82nd Street. The company became one of the city's top real estate firms on sales volume that year and has been among the leaders ever since.

Beverley and Pat consistently attract skilled REALTORS to the company. Many of the firm's agents hold designations from the Gradu-

ate Real Estate Institute or are Certified Real Estate Specialists. During the two-year period ending in 1993, Pat Ham, Inc., REAL-TORS generated $109 million in sales by specializing in the better properties in all price ranges. "We have a house listed for $20,000 and one for $2 million," Beverley explains, "and we like to do everything in between."

BEVERLEY ALBIN, FIRST PRINCIPAL *broker and sales manager, helped Pat Ham, Inc., REALTORS get its start in 1985.*

THE FIRM'S ATTRACTIVE LUBBOCK *headquarters is located on Quaker Avenue, south of the Loop (right).*

PAT HAM, INC., REALTORS
*specializes in the better properties
in all price ranges.*

## MEETING DIVERSE
## CUSTOMER NEEDS

Pat Ham, Inc., REALTORS assists home sellers in a variety of ways. The company employs modern computer technology to generate a 10-page Comparative Market Analysis (CMA) for properties, which helps the REALTOR and the seller determine the best price for the home. The company subsequently develops a cost sheet so that the seller knows exactly what expenses to expect at closing. The company's special expertise resides, however, in the experience of its agents. Pat Ham, Inc., REALTORS advises sellers on steps to take around a home before it is offered for sale so that each property reaches its full price potential.

The firm also specializes in relocations through its aggressive Relocation Department and recently became affiliated with All Points Relocation Services, a referral network that links REALTORS across the United States, Canada, and Mexico. Through All Points, Pat Ham, Inc., REALTORS learns what the customer seeks in a home and assembles portfolios, which show houses listed with the firm

that meet customer requirements. The portfolios include Lubbock Chamber of Commerce material and information on schools, retail shopping, and churches, and are customized by the real estate firm to include special information requested by the customer. The Relocation Department also helps families who are leaving Lubbock obtain information about the communities to which they are relocating.

The Relocation Department is a service to area employers who are interviewing candidates and who want to familiarize their prospects with Lubbock's advantages. Welcoming transfers or potential candidates is one of the things the firm does best. Pat Ham, Inc., REALTORS will send out community materials for employers or provide a grand tour of the community for prospective employees.

### SELLING LUBBOCK

Pat says one reason her firm is successful is because its REALTORS sell more than a house; they sell Lubbock. "We do a lot of PR work for the medical community, or people who come in here for

Texas Tech University, or people who come just to look the city over," she explains.

The firm's friendly enthusiasm radiates back to the community. Beverley, for example, was Lubbock's Salesman of the Year in 1991 because of her community service and active involvement in the Lubbock Association of REALTORS, where she is currently treasurer. Beverley also is active in United Way.

Pat Ham, Inc., REALTORS generates more than sales when it comes to Lubbock. The company is a frequent benefactor for the Lubbock Symphony Orchestra, the Junior League, the Heart Fund, the March of Dimes, the Lubbock Children's Home, the South Plains Kidney Foundation, and a long list of civic and charitable organizations.

Adds Beverley, "We really do believe in Lubbock, and when we're asked to show Lubbock to a candidate for relocation it's easy for us to do because we love Lubbock."

ACCORDING TO PAT HAM, THE *company's REALTORS sell more than a house; they sell Lubbock.*

# PHOTOGRAPHERS

**KRISTOPHER BAILEY**, originally from Houston, is a photocommunications major at Texas Tech University. He also works for the university in the photographic services branch of the Office of News and Publications. Bailey specializes in commercial, studio, and abstract photography, and plans to continue his studies at the Brooks Institute of Photography after his graduation.

**JEREMY ALAN CHESNUTT** is studying photocommunications at Texas Tech University. He works for the university newspaper, *The University Daily*, and has also done some promotional work for Lubbock-area bands. Chesnutt specializes in landscape photography and enjoys traveling and photographing new areas.

**PAUL THOMAS CROUSE**, originally from Dallas, has a bachelor of science degree in radio, television, and film from West Texas A&M. A freelance photographer specializing in video and black-and-white photography, he is also pursuing a master's degree in photography. In 1993 Crouse won a silver Addy award in industrial/educational films or programs.

**RICK DINGUS** is a native of Appleton City, Missouri. A professor in the art department at Texas Tech University, he has a bachelor's degree from the University of California at Santa Barbara and both a master's degree and a master of fine arts degree from the University of New Mexico. Dingus' photography has been shown in more than 100 group exhibits and in 17 solo exhibits. His work is included in numerous public collections, including the Museum of Modern Art and the Metropolitan Museum of Art in New York City, the Bibliotheque Nationale in Paris, and the Australian National Gallery of Art.

**KEN HALPAIN** is an electrical engineering student at Texas Tech. Born and raised in Lubbock, he conducts contract electrical repair and is active with the U.S. Navy Reserves. Halpain is also interested in motorcycles and motor racing.

**AL HENDERSON**, born in Brownfield, Texas, has lived in Lubbock since he was four years old. He is a student at Texas Tech and operates Henderson Photo, where he specializes in sports, high school athletic, and dirt-track auto racing photography. His work has been published in the *Slatonite* (Slaton, Texas) and in a number of racing magazines, including *World Karting*, *Racing News*, and *Karter News*. Henderson has been the track photographer for the West Texas Speedway for seven years and is currently at work on a documentary series on the emotions of high school athletes, coaches, and fans.

**VAUGHN HENDRIE**, originally from Overton, Texas, has lived in the Lubbock area since 1969. He attended Kilgore Junior College and went on to North Texas State University, where he majored in journalism and advertising. Hendrie also attended the Texas School of Photography, the Georgia School of Photography, and the Winona School. He currently operates Hendrie Photography, a studio specializing in wedding photography and portraiture.

**VAL HILDRETH**, a lifelong Lubbockite, operates Southwest Photo in Lubbock. She has a bachelor's degree in photography and is working toward a master of fine arts degree. Hildreth specializes in wilderness adventure and cave photography as well as multi-image and video production. She has also been contracted to do environmental photomonitoring, and she regularly produces documentation for the National Park Service, the U.S. Forest Service, and the Bureau of Land Management.

**ARTIE LIMMER** serves as assistant director and manager of photographic services in the Office of News and Publications at Texas Tech University. In that position, he oversees both staff and student photographers who cover the main university campus and the Health Sciences Center campus. Limmer has won numerous gold medals in CASE district and national competitions and was named the CASE University Photographer of the Year in 1993. His work has appeared in numerous periodicals, including *Texas Monthly*, *Newsweek*, *Texas Highways*, and *Scientific American*. He holds a bachelor's degree from Texas Tech University.

**HARVEY MADISON** is a lifelong West Texan. He has both a bachelor's degree in psychology and a master's degree in education and currently operates Madison Photographics, a commercial photography studio. Madison also teaches photography courses. "I have been in love with the skies of West Texas all my life," he says. "I enjoy astronomy, meteorology, and I am a private pilot and a balloonist. Clouds and stars turn me on."

**MARK C. MAMAWAL**, originally from Upstate New York, has lived in Lubbock since 1982. He earned a bachelor of arts degree in photocommunications from Texas Tech University and now works in the photographic services division of the university's Office of News and Publications. Mamawal specializes in promotional and commercial photography and has won several regional CASE gold medals. His work has also been published in both *Texas Monthly* and *Texas Parks and Wildlife*.

**DARREN POORE** earned a bachelor of fine arts degree in photography and printmaking from Texas Tech University. After working for six years in the university's Office of News and Publications, Poore now does freelance photography. His specialty is portraiture. "My images are about people, human interaction, and subtle moments in time," Poore says.

▶ AL HENDERSON

MILTON "MAC" ROWLEY, M.D., is a plastic surgeon originally from Clovis, New Mexico. He enjoys shooting landscape images and has attended numerous photography workshops with Ansel Adams, Paul Caponegro, John Sexton, Bruce Barnbaum, and others. Rowley's work has appeared in *New Mexico* magazine and is featured in numerous private collections. He also recently began a series of portraits of western artists and poets.

CORY SINKLIER, originally from San Antonio, has lived in Lubbock since 1991. He is a student at Texas Tech University where he is majoring in photocommunications with a minor in art. He is also a photographer for the university's newspaper, *The University Daily*. Sinklier is the son of a photographer and has enjoyed photography since a very early age.

SHARON M. STEINMAN graduated magna cum laude from Texas Tech University in 1994 with a bachelor's degree in photocommunications. She worked for the campus newspaper, *The University Daily*, while in school and was named its Outstanding Photographer in 1991, 1992, and 1994. She also won the Associated Collegiate Press third-place News Picture of the Year award in 1993 and second-place Sports Picture of the Year award in 1992. She is a member of the National Press Photographers Association and has worked freelance for Texas Tech's sports information office.

JON Q. THOMPSON, a native Lubbockite, photographs for JQT Visual Productions in Lubbock. He has a bachelor's degree from the Brooks Institute of Photography and both a master's degree and a photographic craftsman's degree from the Professional Photographers of America. Thompson specializes in commercial/advertising photography and presentation graphics.

TINA THOMPSON, originally from Tulsa, Oklahoma, moved to Lubbock in 1987. A certified professional photographer, she photographs for JQT Visual Productions in Lubbock. Thompson specializes in fine art portraiture and other photographic art.

GRANT E. WARNER, originally from Houston, is a recent graduate of Texas Tech University. He now does computer modeling, graphics, and model building for Three/Architecture, Inc. in Dallas, and his photography and design work have been published in *Elevation*. Warner is a self-described traveler, aperture addict, Tex-Mex junkie, avid Trekker, deft designer, foreign film fan, soccer player, and "aspiring" writer.

# INDEX TO SPONSORS